Presenting:

BLACK AND WHITE NIGHT

GET OUT YOUR FLASHLIGHT FOR OUR BLACK AND WHITE NIGHT!

WORDS & ART BY: BRIANNA DAVIS

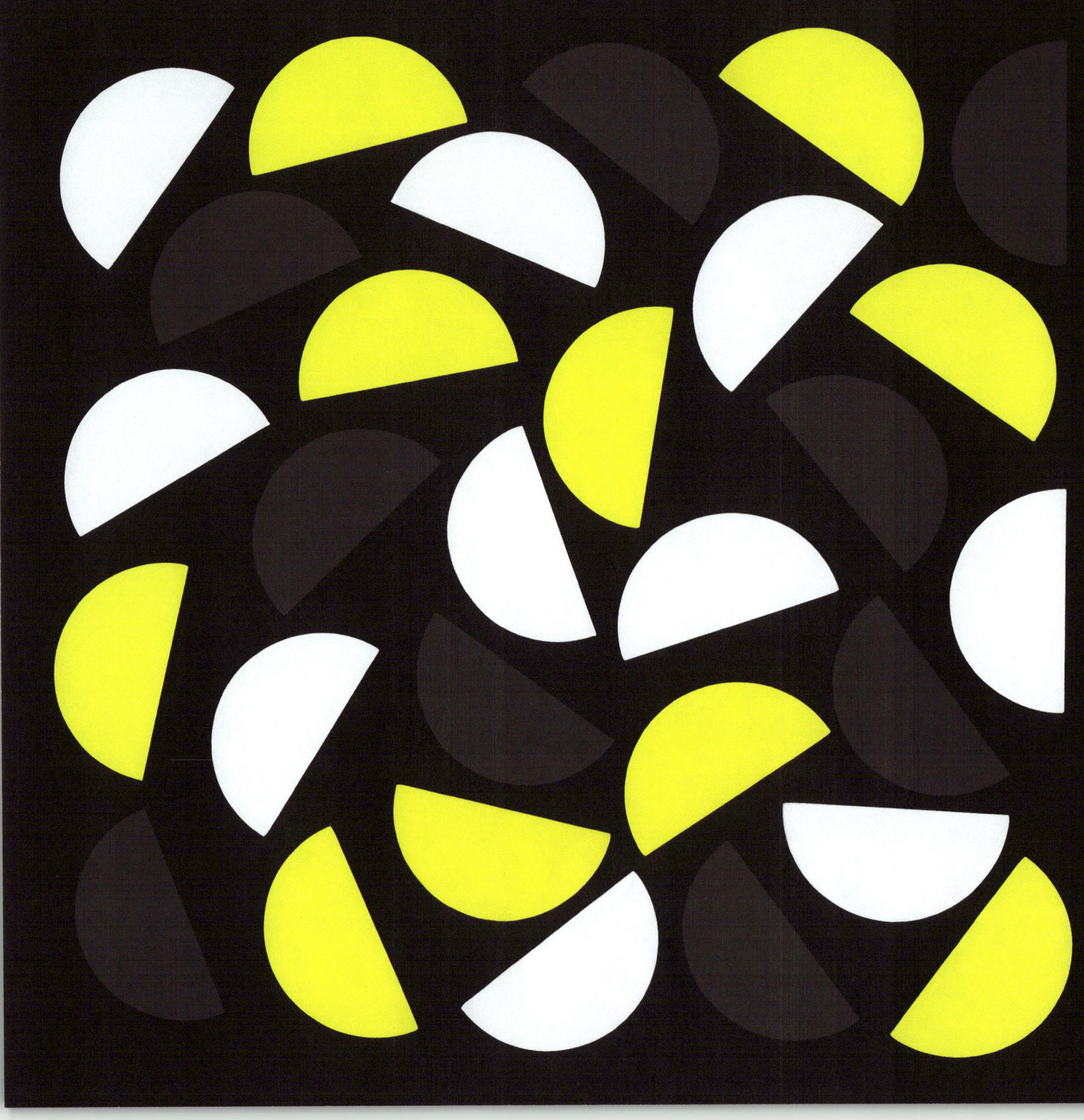

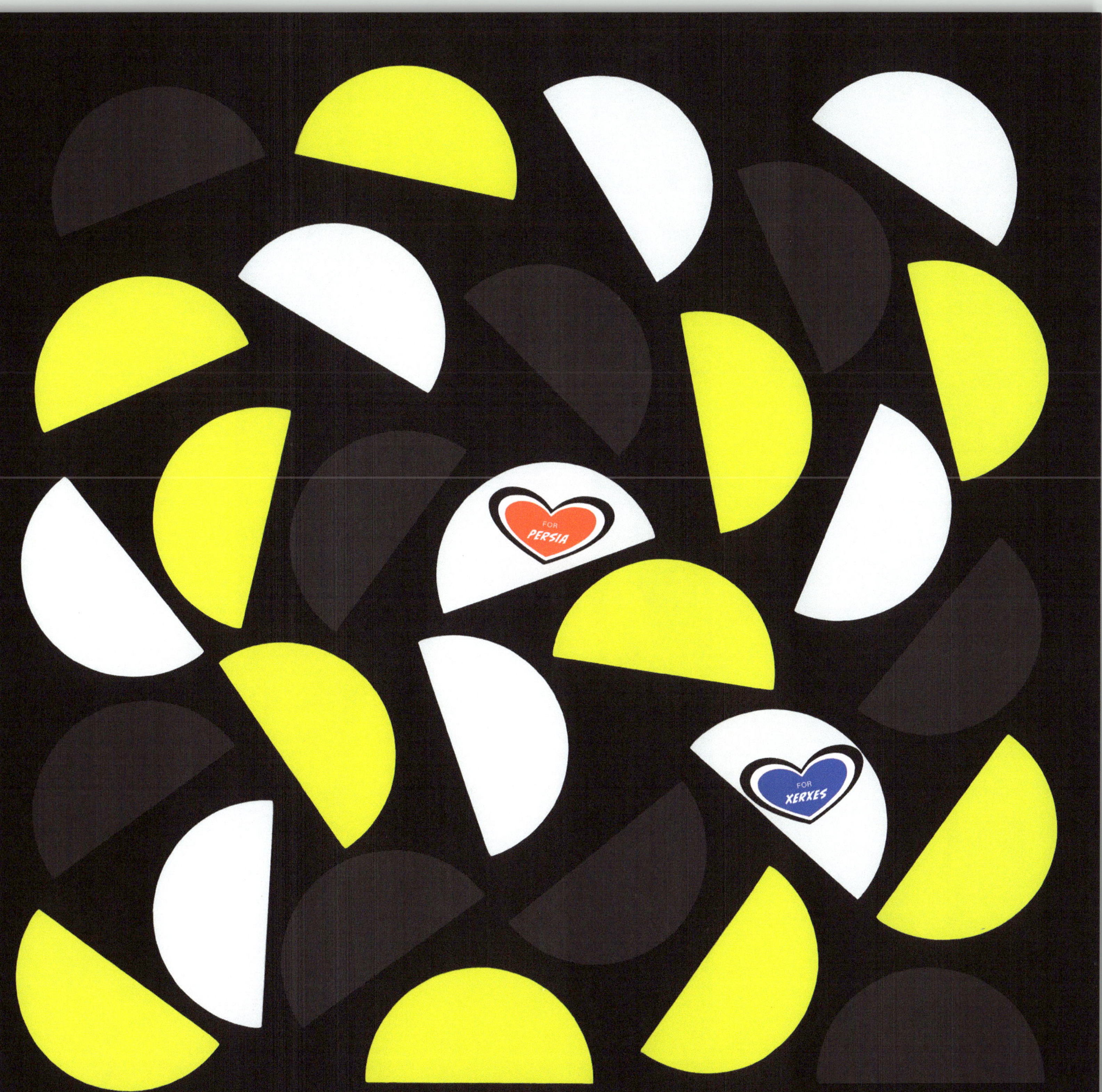
FOR PERSIA
FOR XERXES

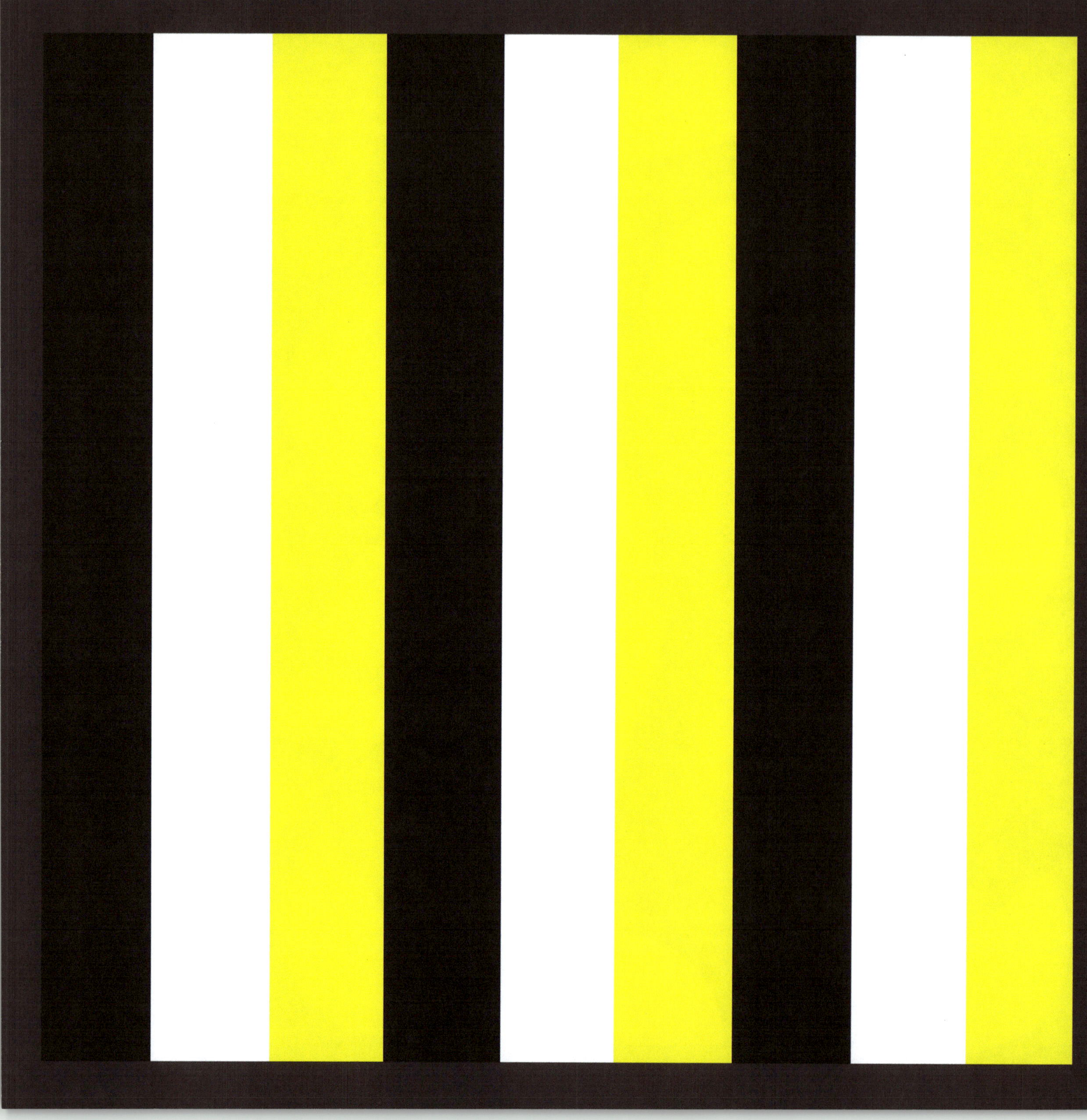

BLACK AND WHITE

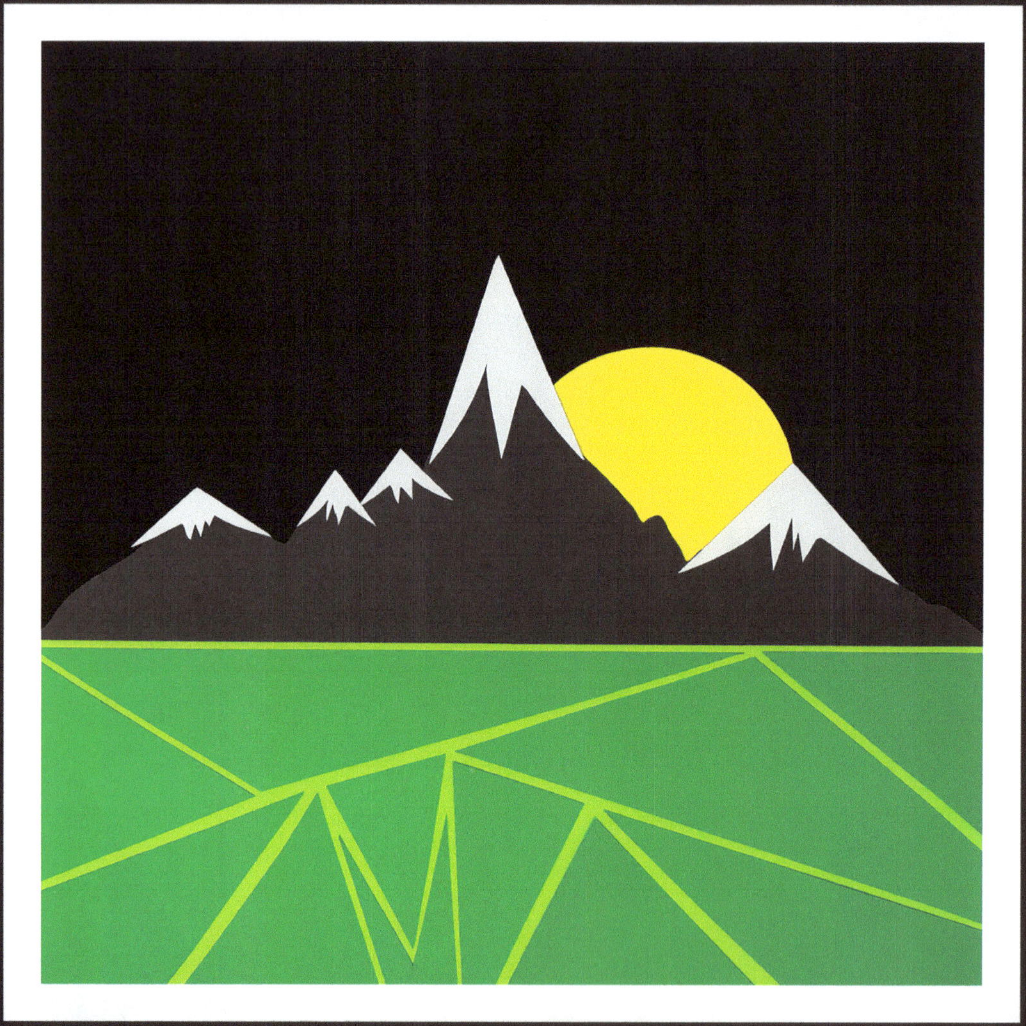

WHEN THE SUN GOES DOWN,
IT'S CALLED NIGHT...

WHICH THEN BEGINS THE ABSENCE OF LIGHT!

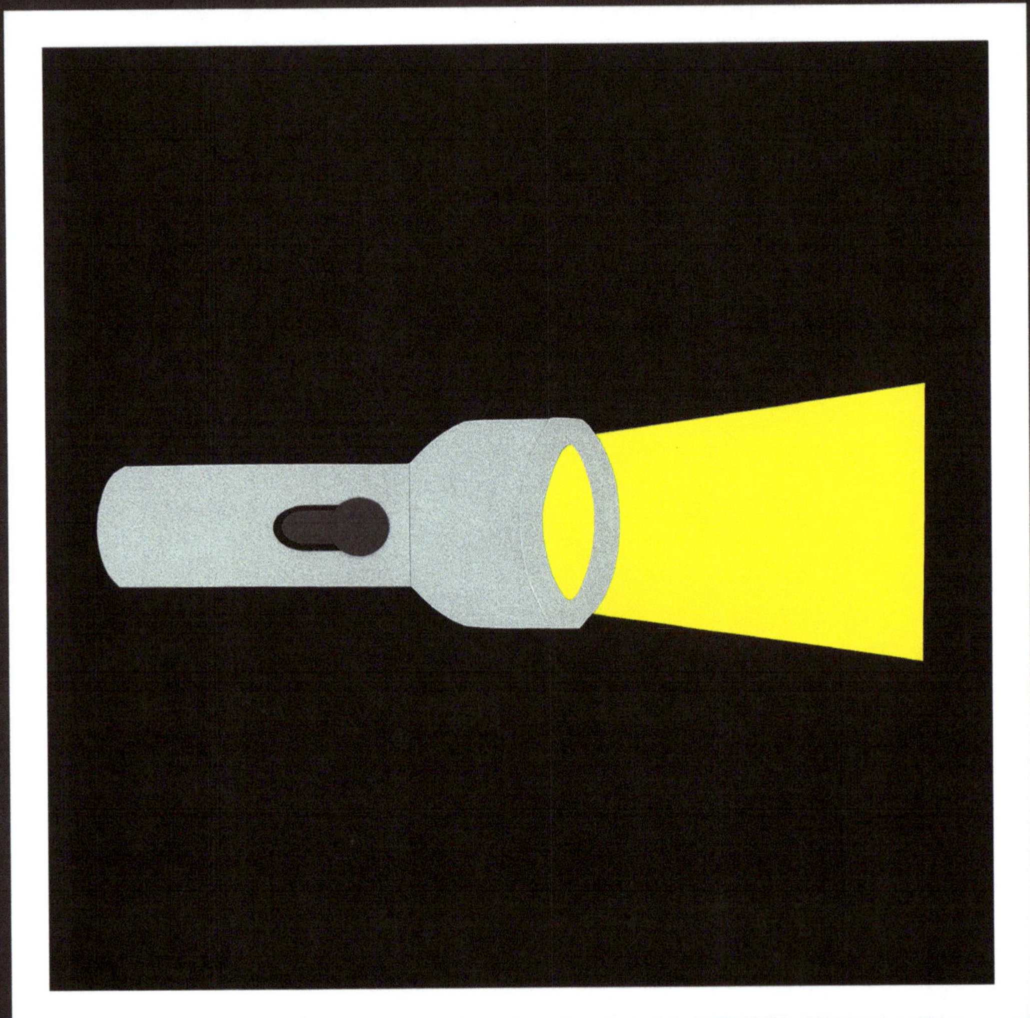

AT NIGHT, WE CAN SEE THINGS
BEST WITH A FLASHLIGHT!

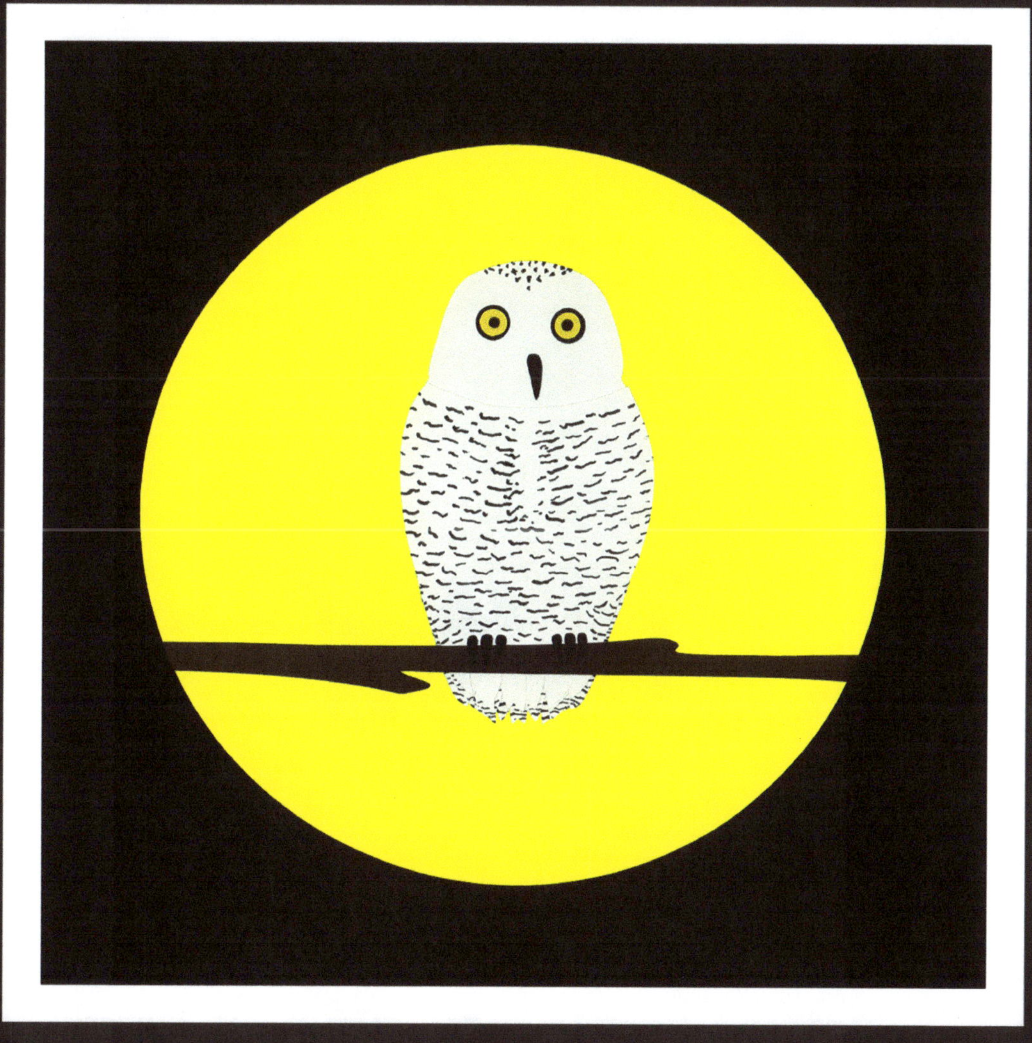

WE HEAR A HOWL,
AND SEE AN OWL!

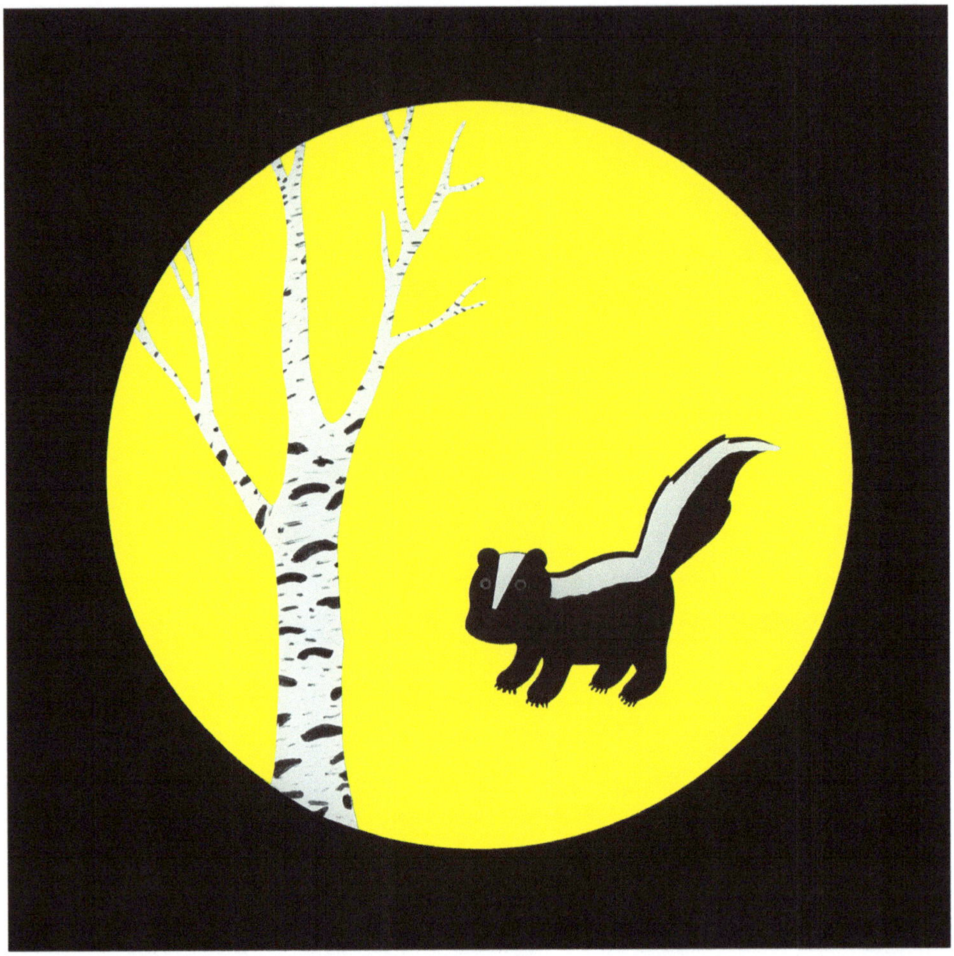

AHEAD I SEE A BIRCH TREE!
WAIT, IS THAT BABY SKUNK
LOOKING AT ME!?

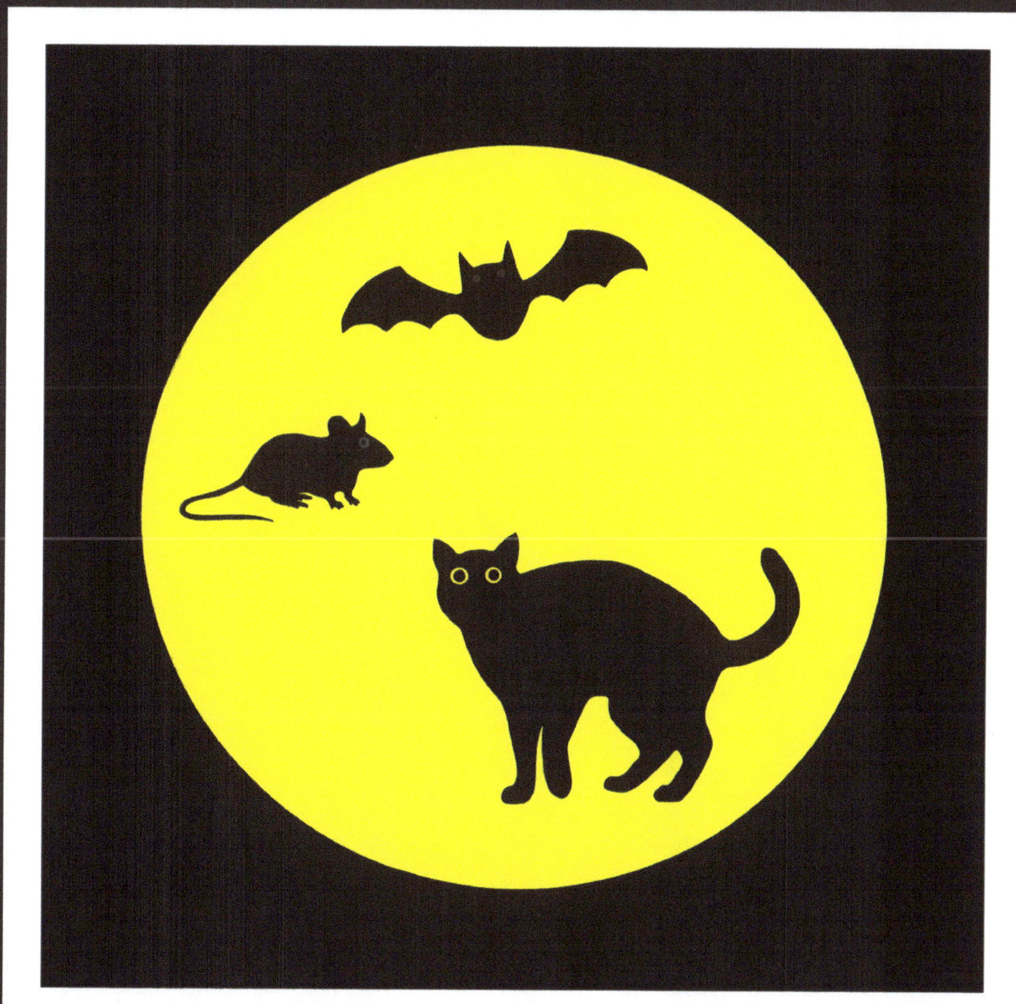

TO MY RIGHT ARE SOME THINGS THAT CAN GIVE A FRIGHT:

A BAT, A RAT, AND A BLACK CAT!

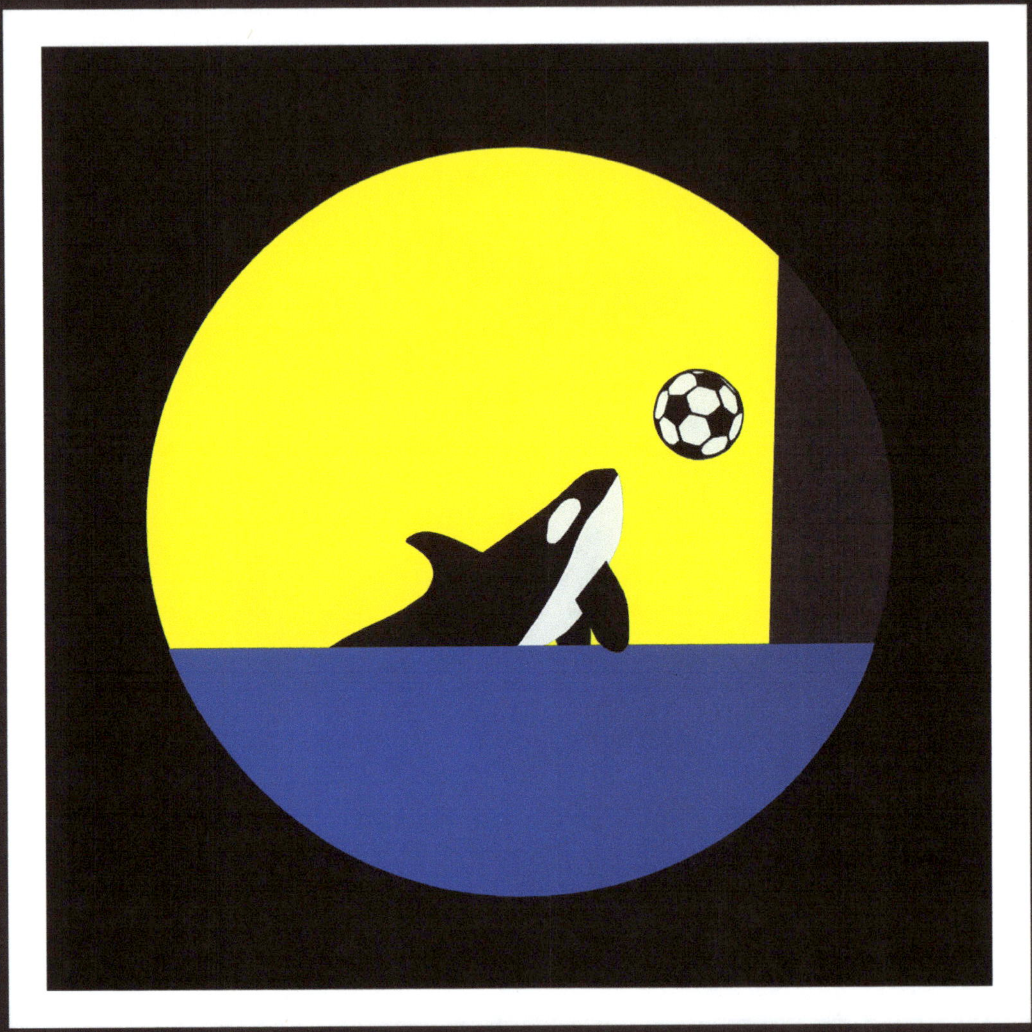

AS WE GO NEAR THE OCEAN, THERE'S A BIT OF COMMOTION:

A WHALE IS BOUNCING A SOCCER BALL OFF THE WALL!

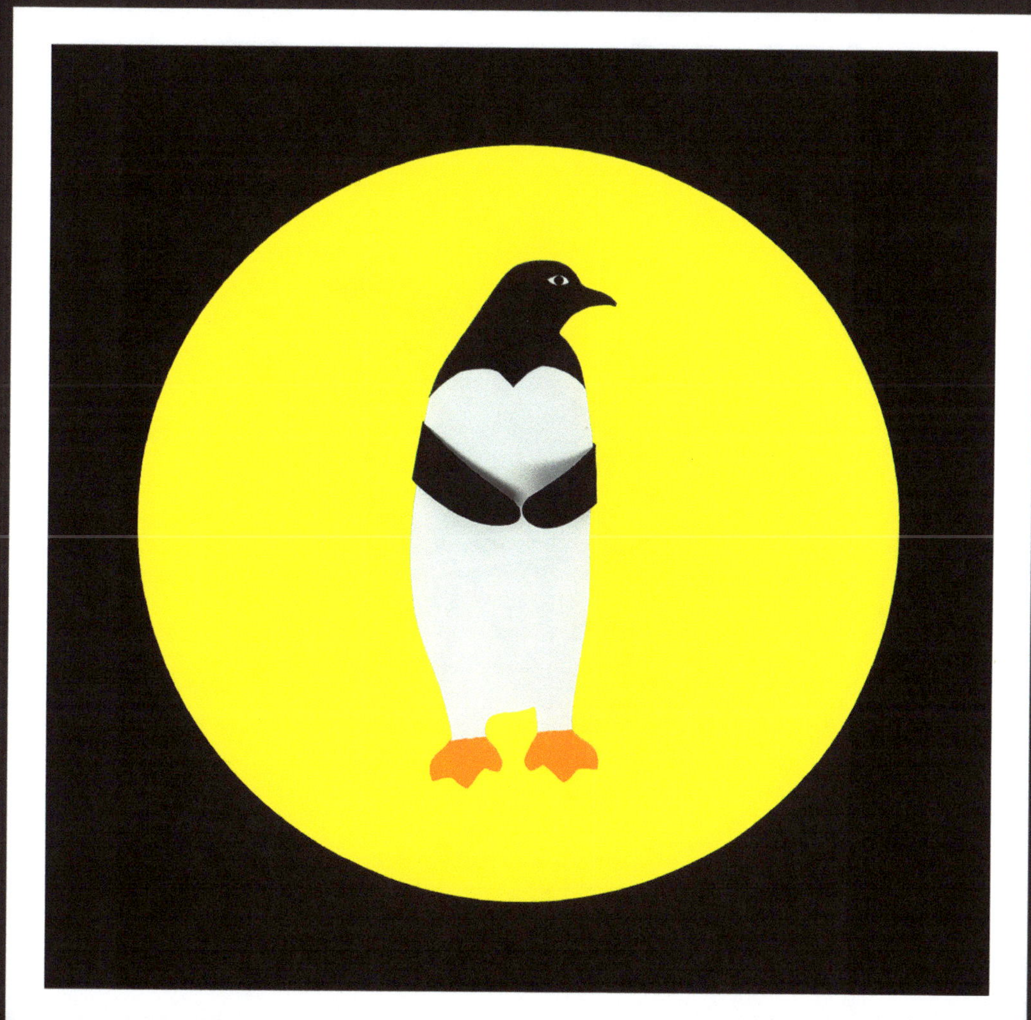

AS WE GO BACK TO LAND, A PENGUIN CLAPS ITS HANDS...

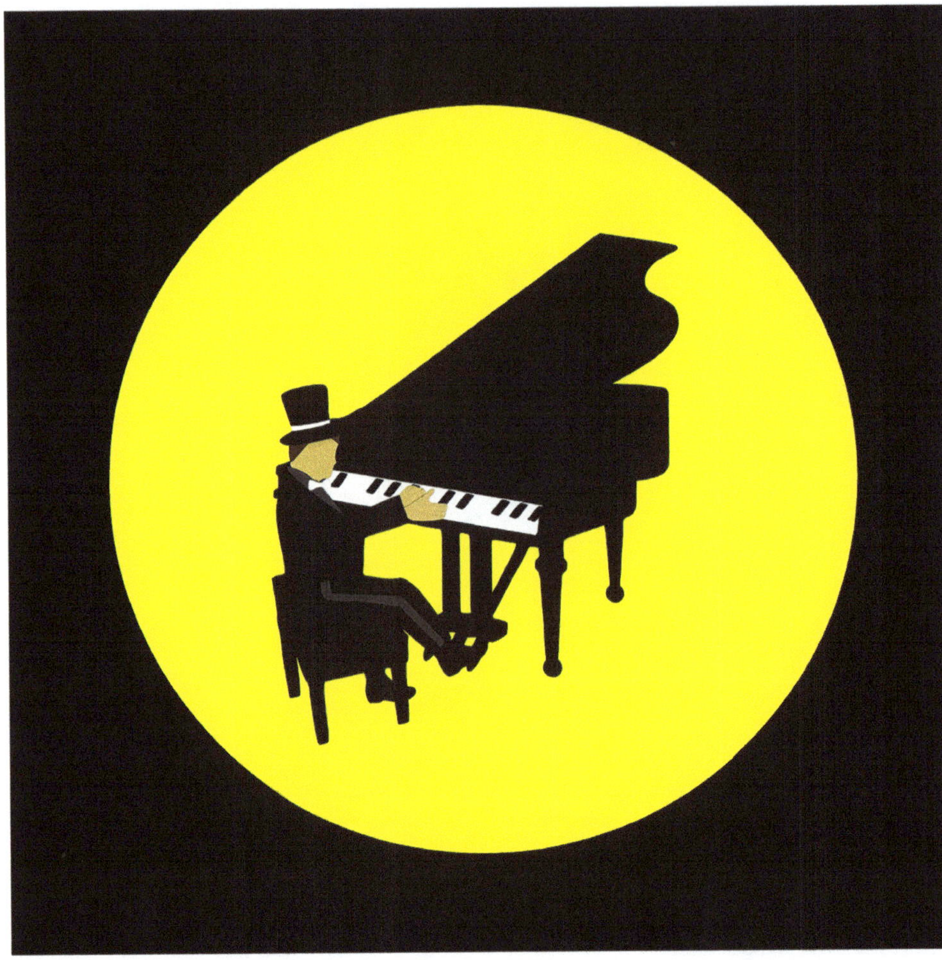

AS A MAN IN A TUXEDO
PLAYS THE PIANO!

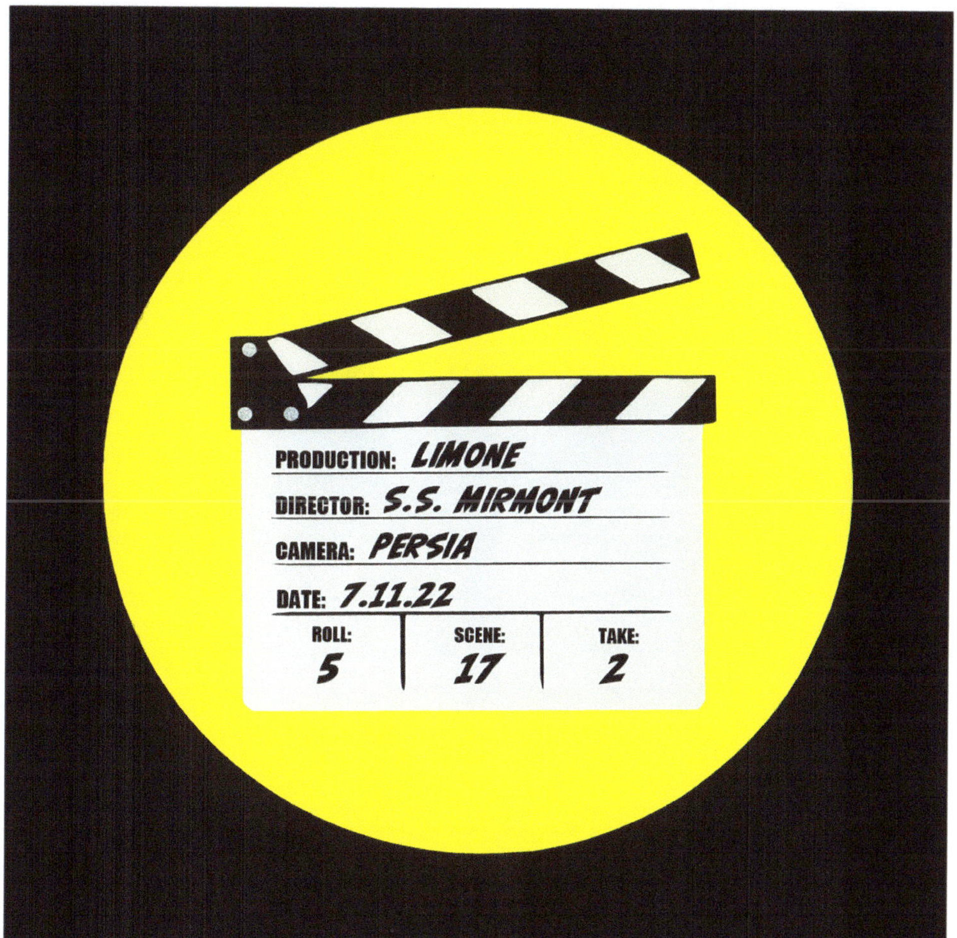

WOW, A FILM SLATE; THIS MOVIE SOUNDS GREAT!

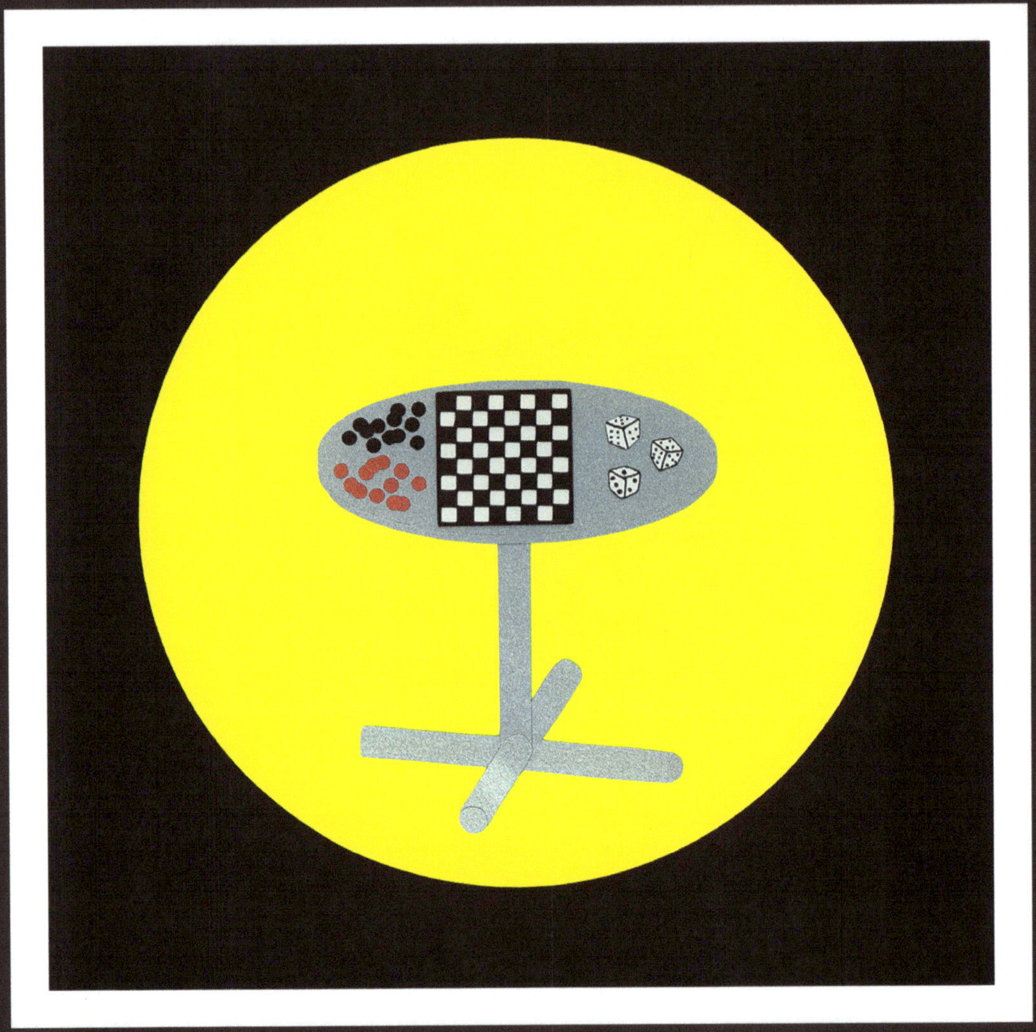

OH LOOK, A CHECKERBOARD
AND SOME DICE...

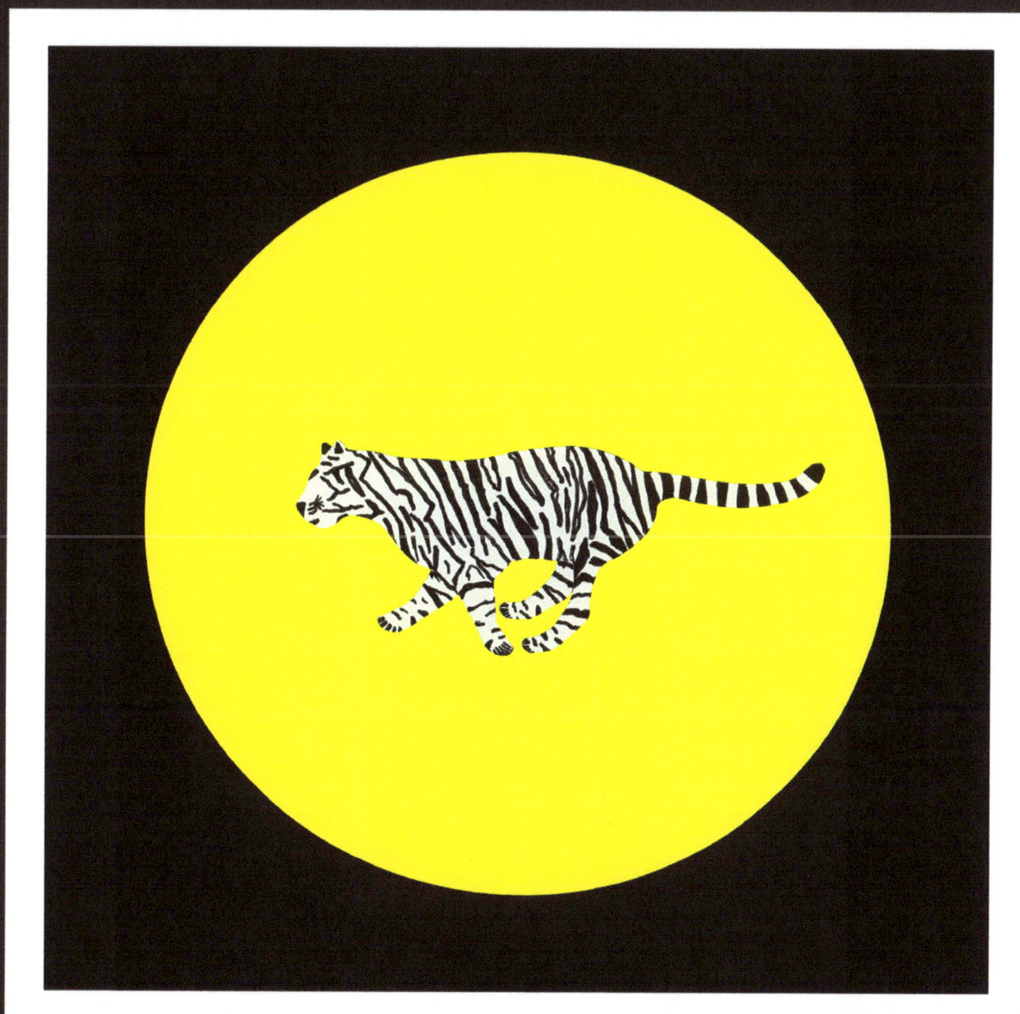

I HOPE THE WHITE TIGER
RUNNING THIS WAY IS NICE!

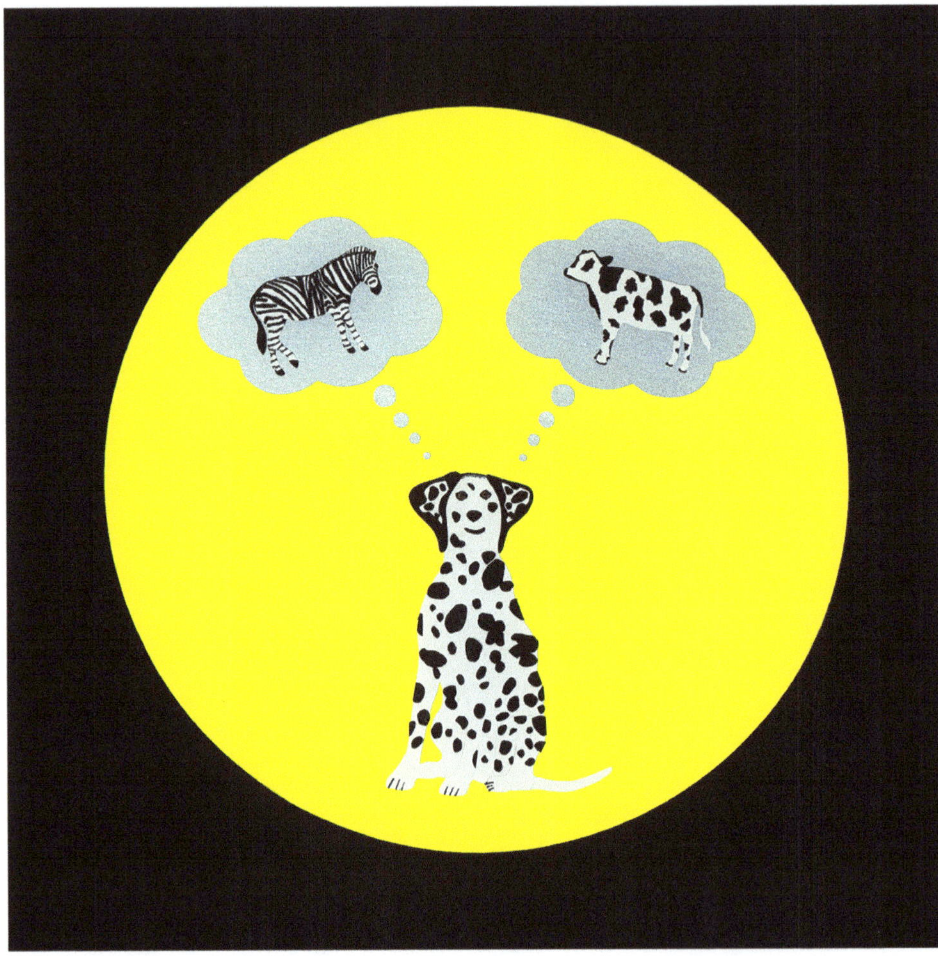

ZEBRAS HAVE STRIPES, COWS HAVE SPOTS,
DALMATIANS HAVE LOTS OF DOTS!

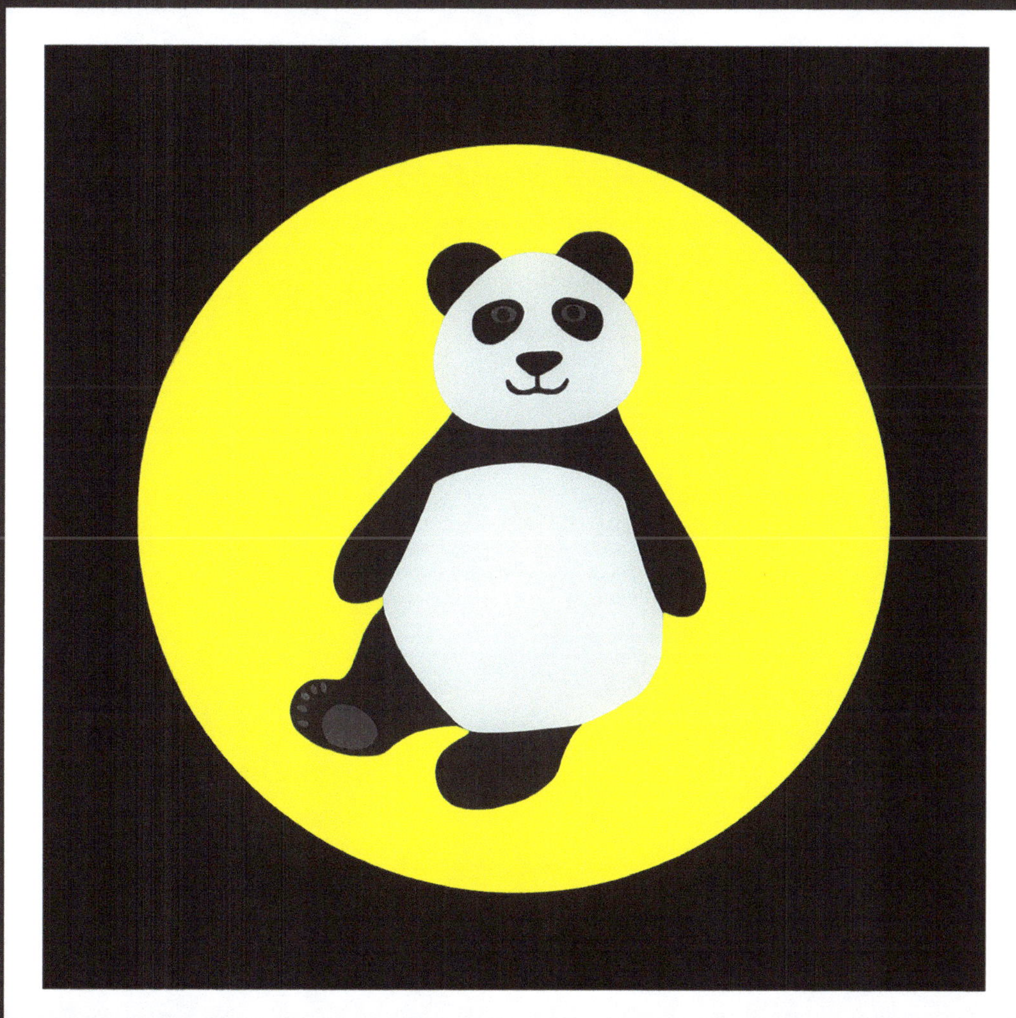

PANDAS ARE THE PERFECT PLACE TO END;
THEY'RE A CUTE LITTLE FRIEND!

LET'S REVIEW WHAT YOU UNCOVERED, AND WHAT WE DISCOVERED IS BLACK AND WHITE!

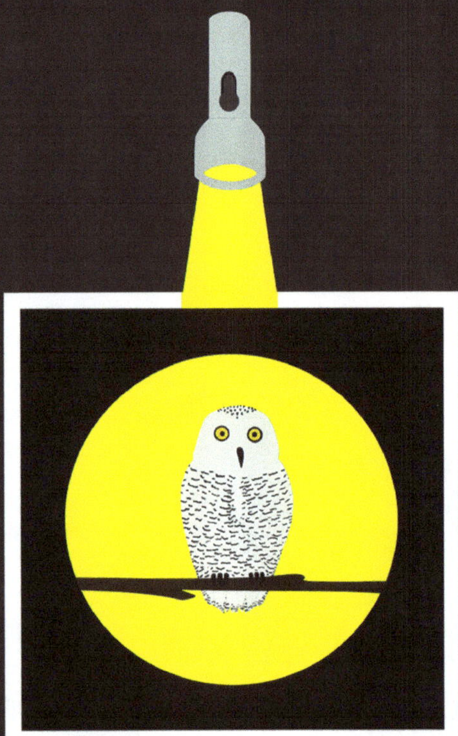

SNOWY OWL!

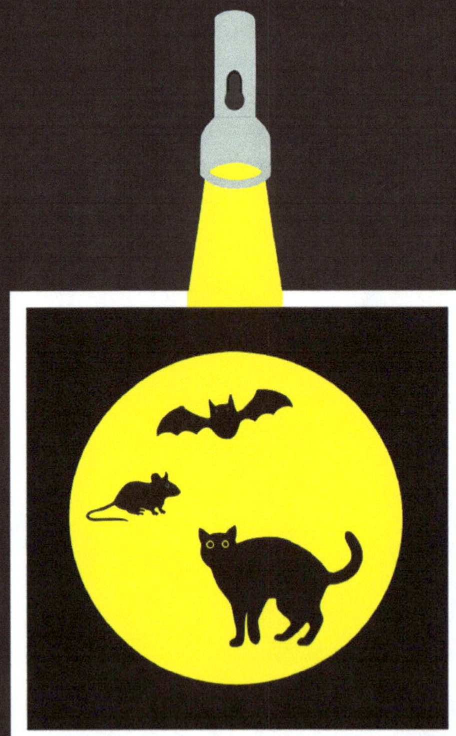

BAT, RAT, CAT!

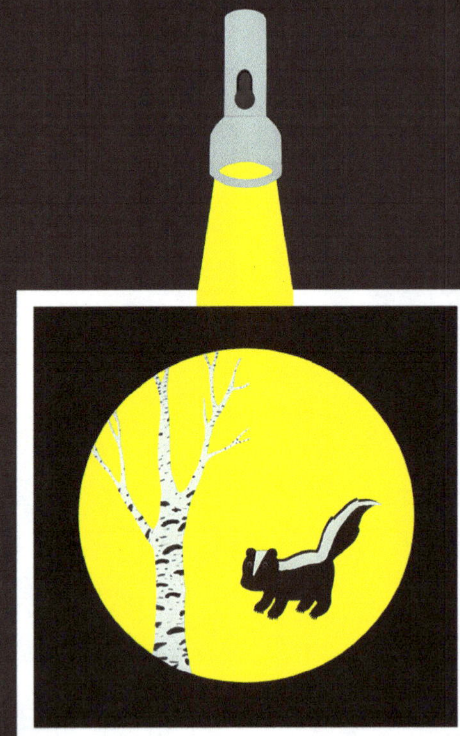

BIRCH TREE, BABY SKUNK!

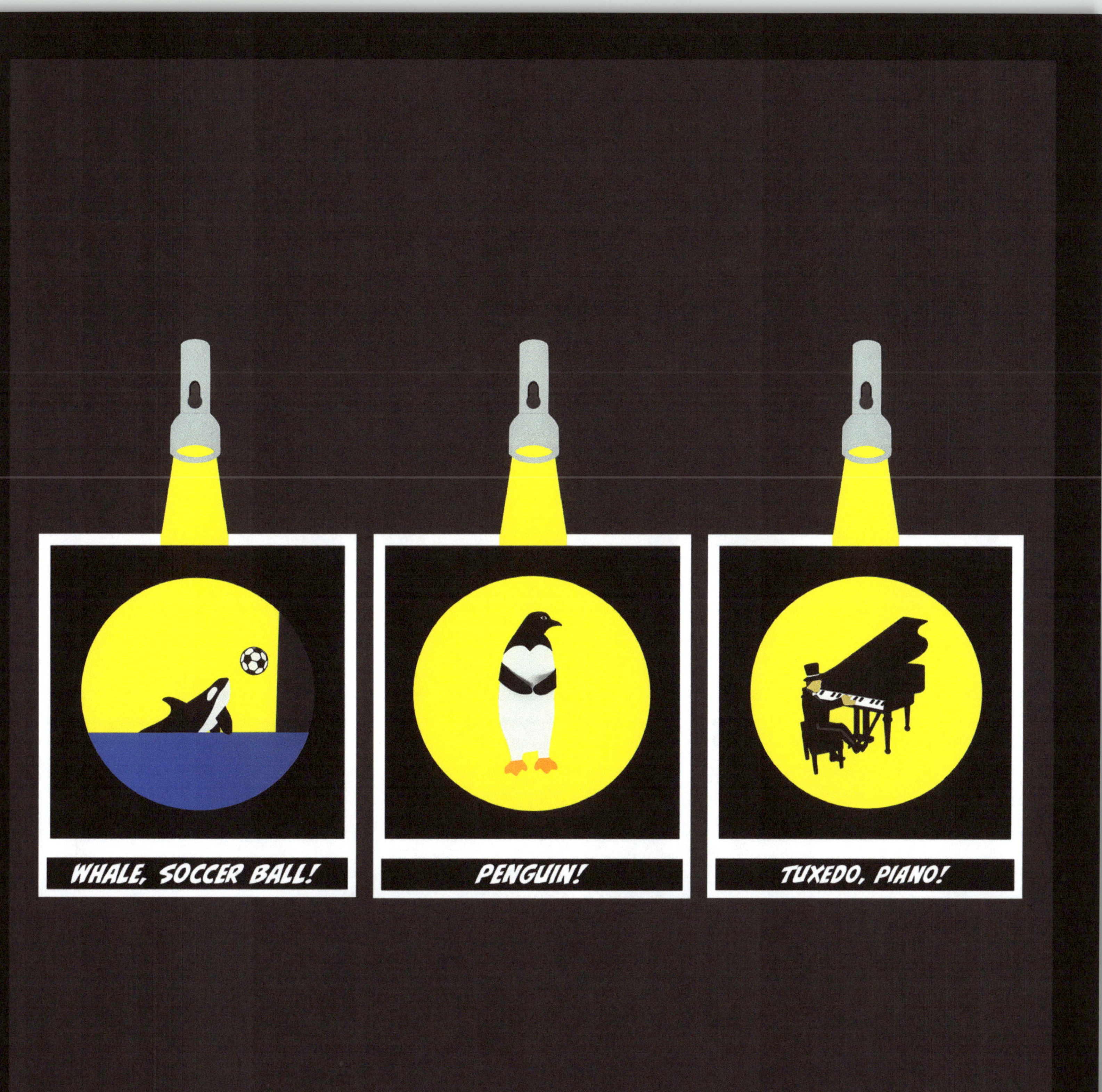
WHALE, SOCCER BALL!
PENGUIN!
TUXEDO, PIANO!

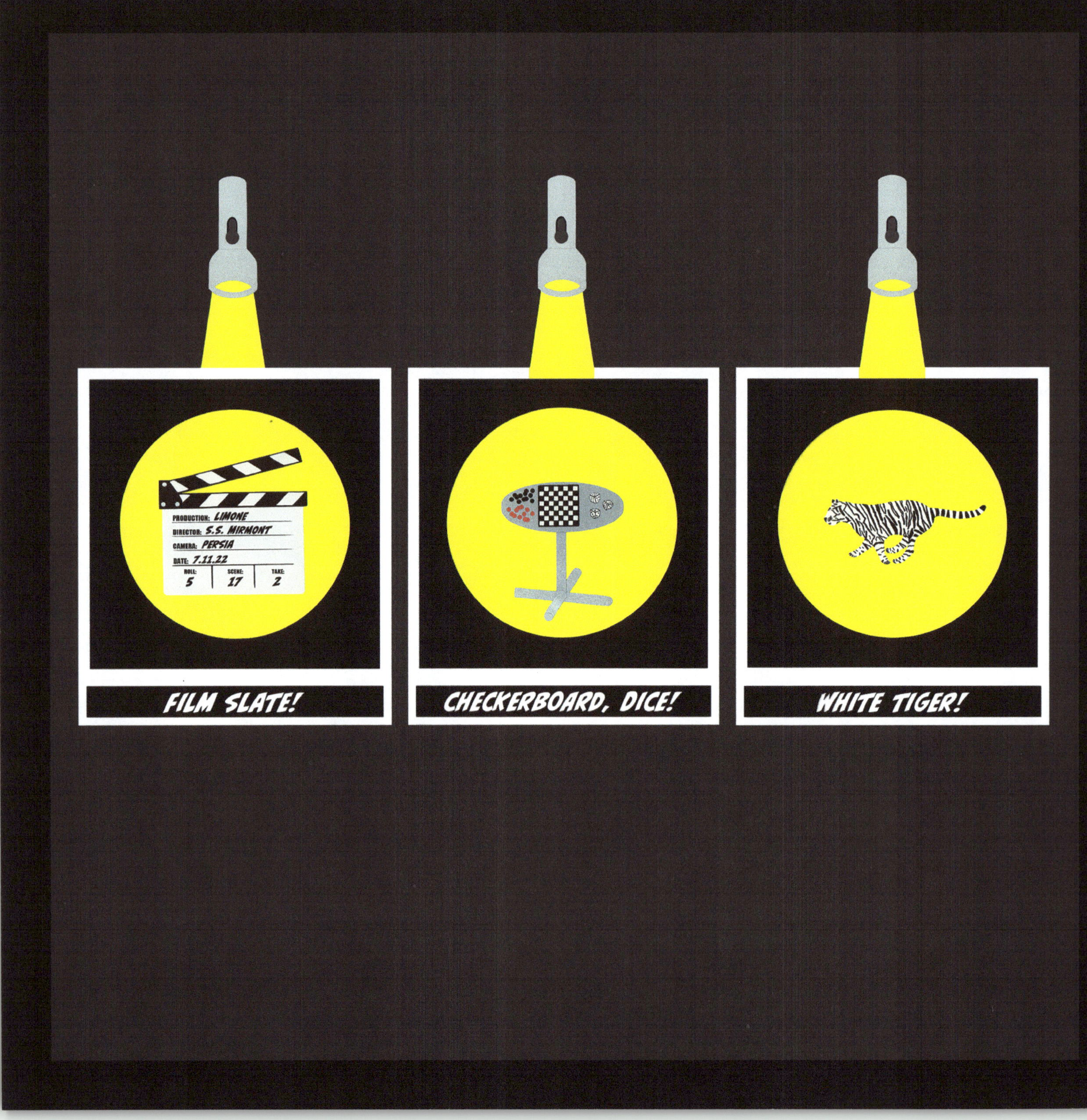
PRODUCTION: LIMONE
DIRECTOR: S.S. MIRMONT
CAMERA: PERSIA
DATE: 7.11.22
ROLL: 5
SCENE: 17
TAKE: 2
FILM SLATE!
CHECKERBOARD, DICE!
WHITE TIGER!

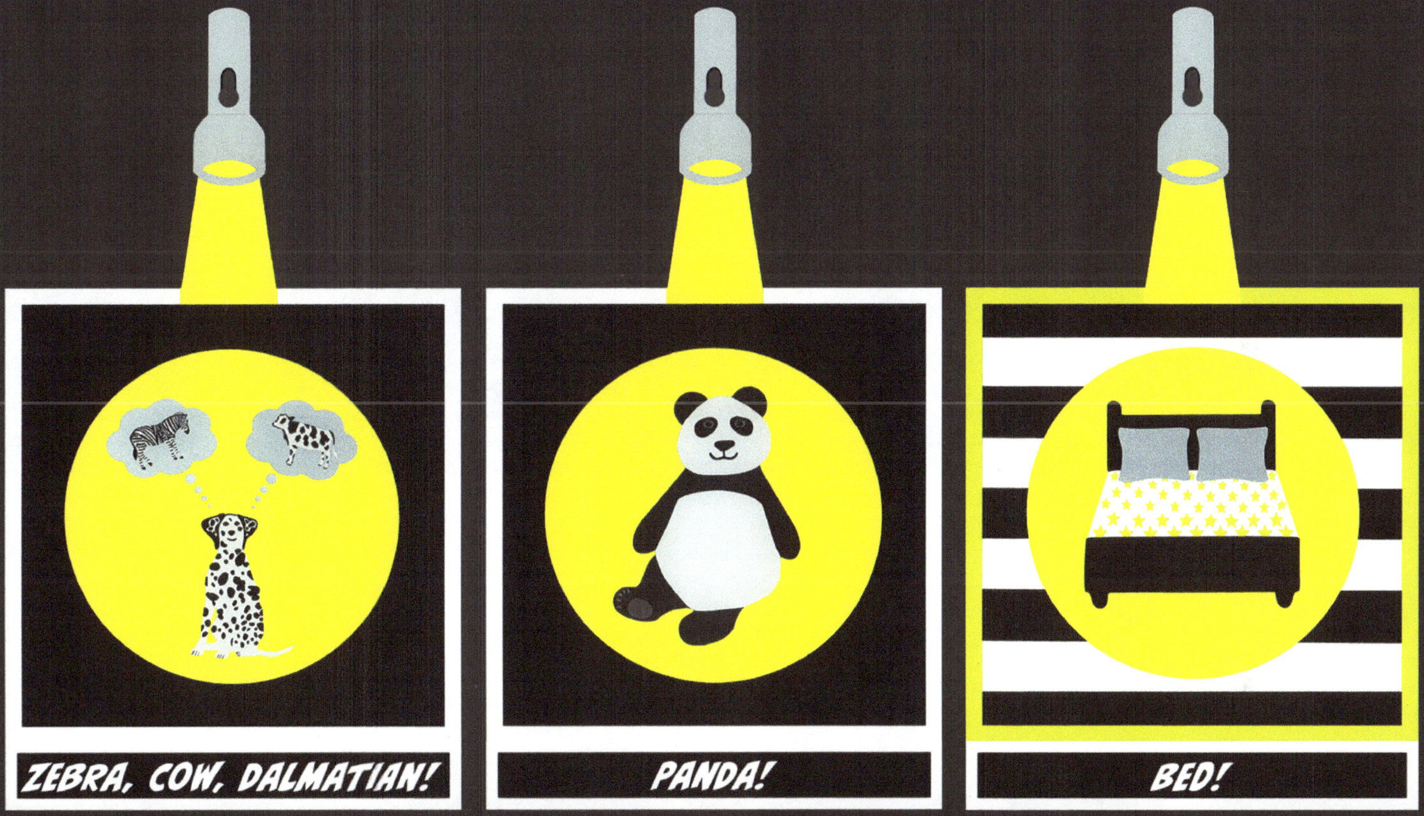

NICE JOB, AND NOW WE'RE THROUGH.
ISN'T IT FUN TO LEARN SOMETHING NEW!

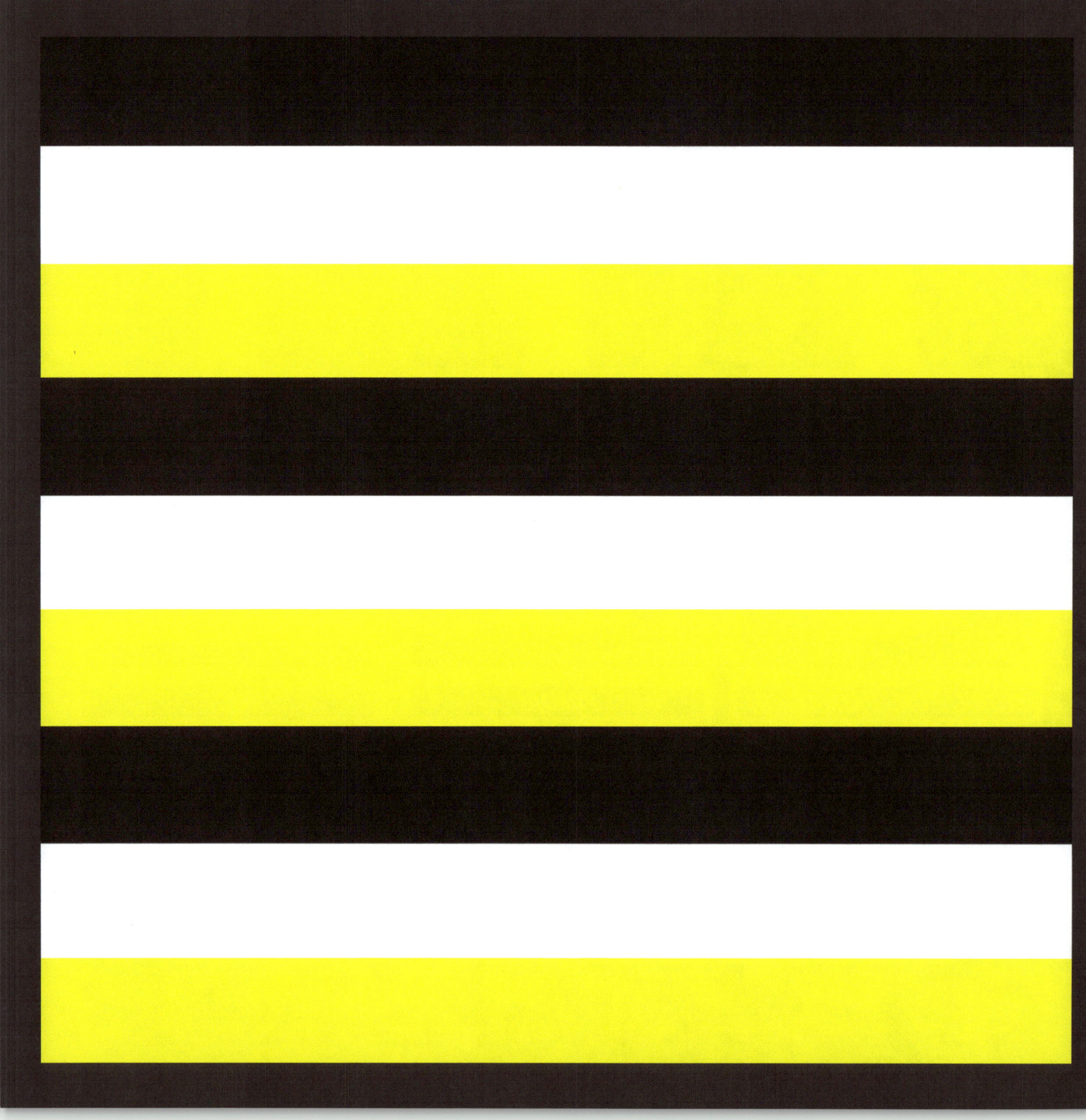

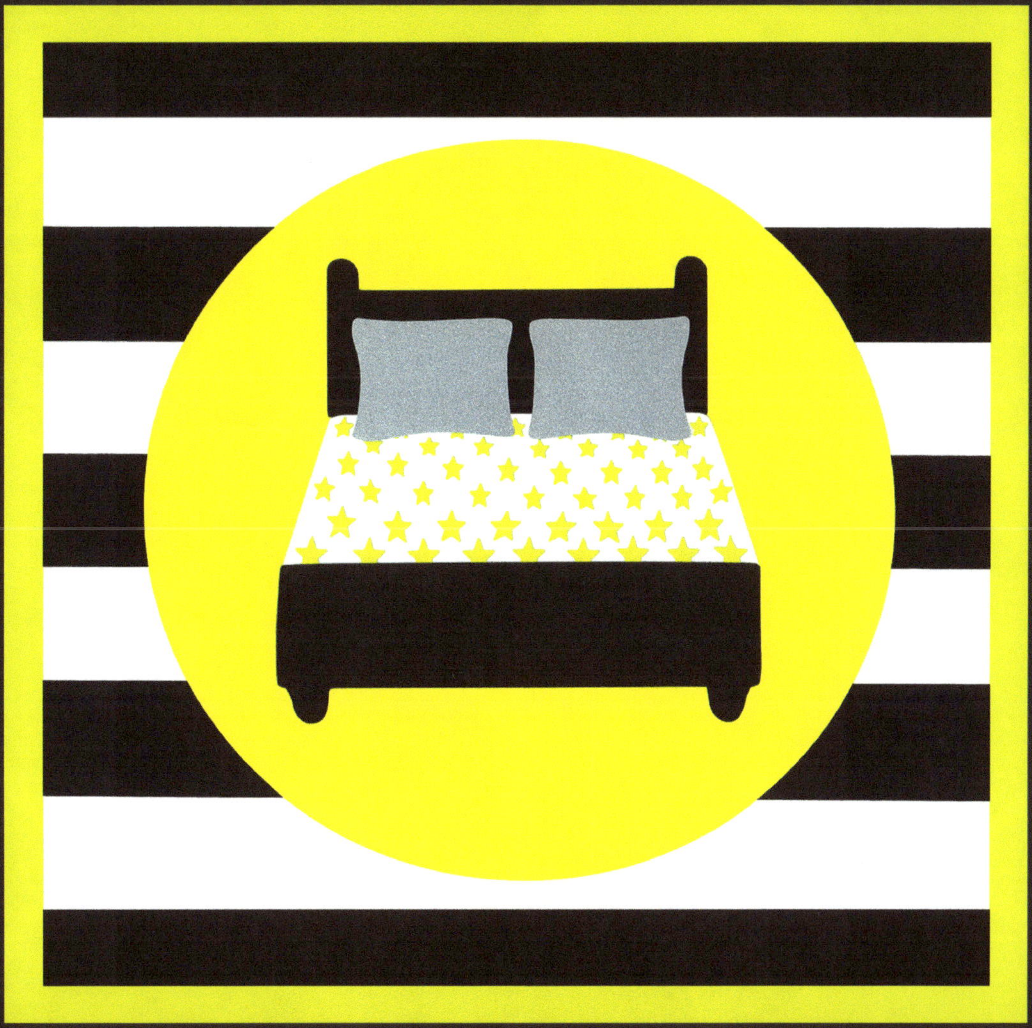

THUS CONCLUDES OUR BLACK AND WHITE NIGHT;

WE HOPE YOU ENJOYED THIS BOOK AND SLEEP TIGHT!

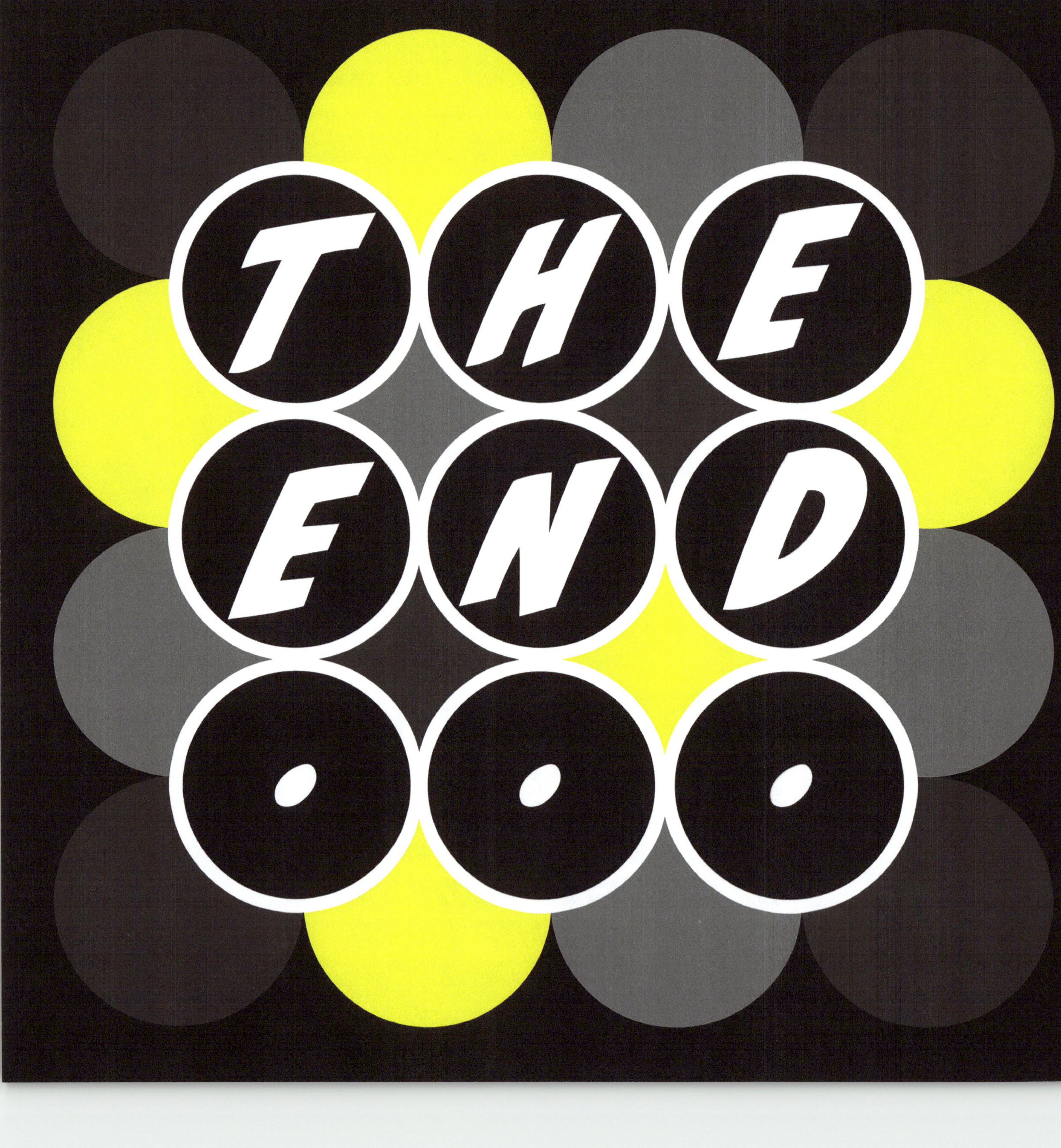
THE
END
...

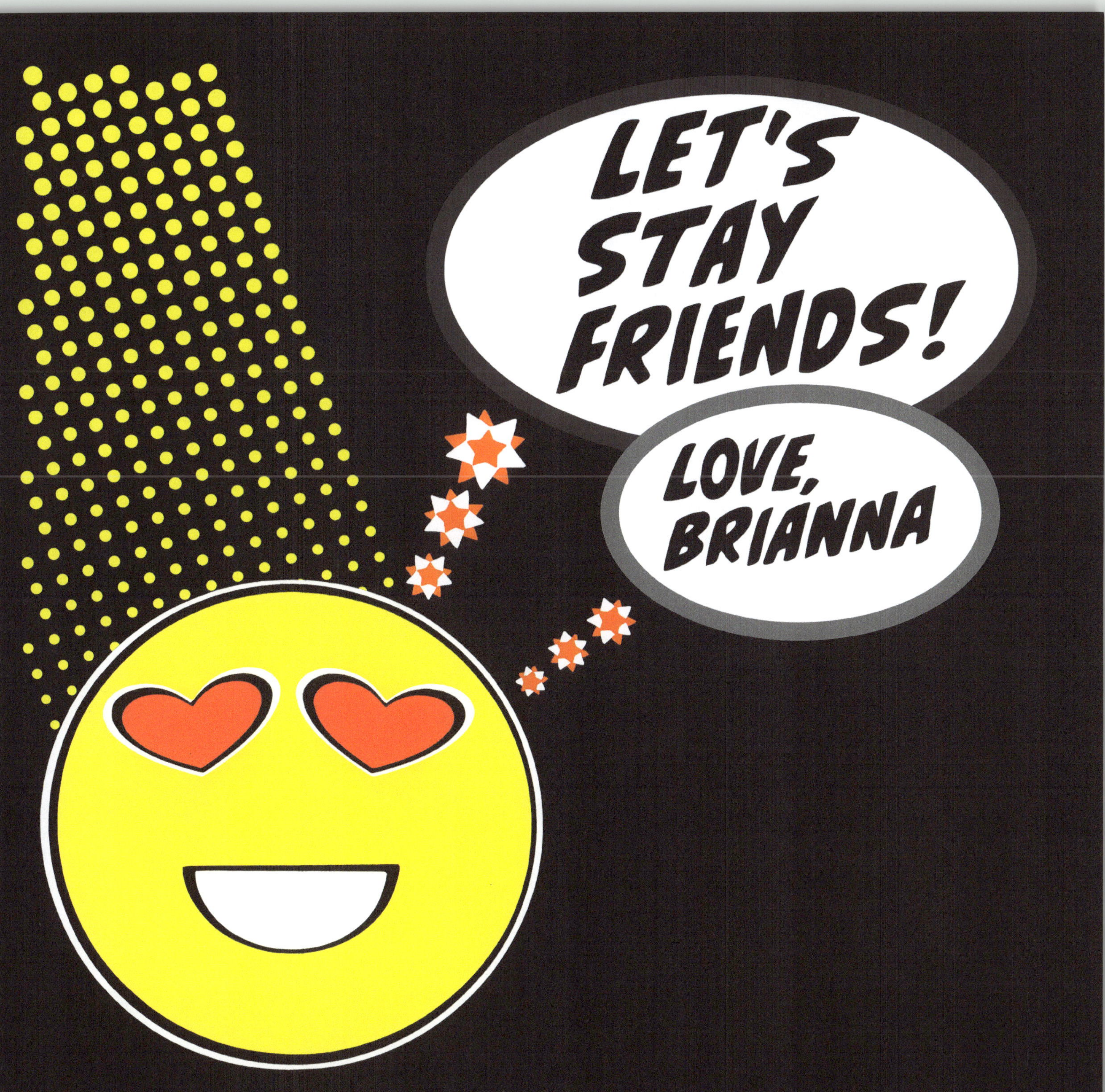
LET'S STAY FRIENDS!
LOVE, BRIANNA

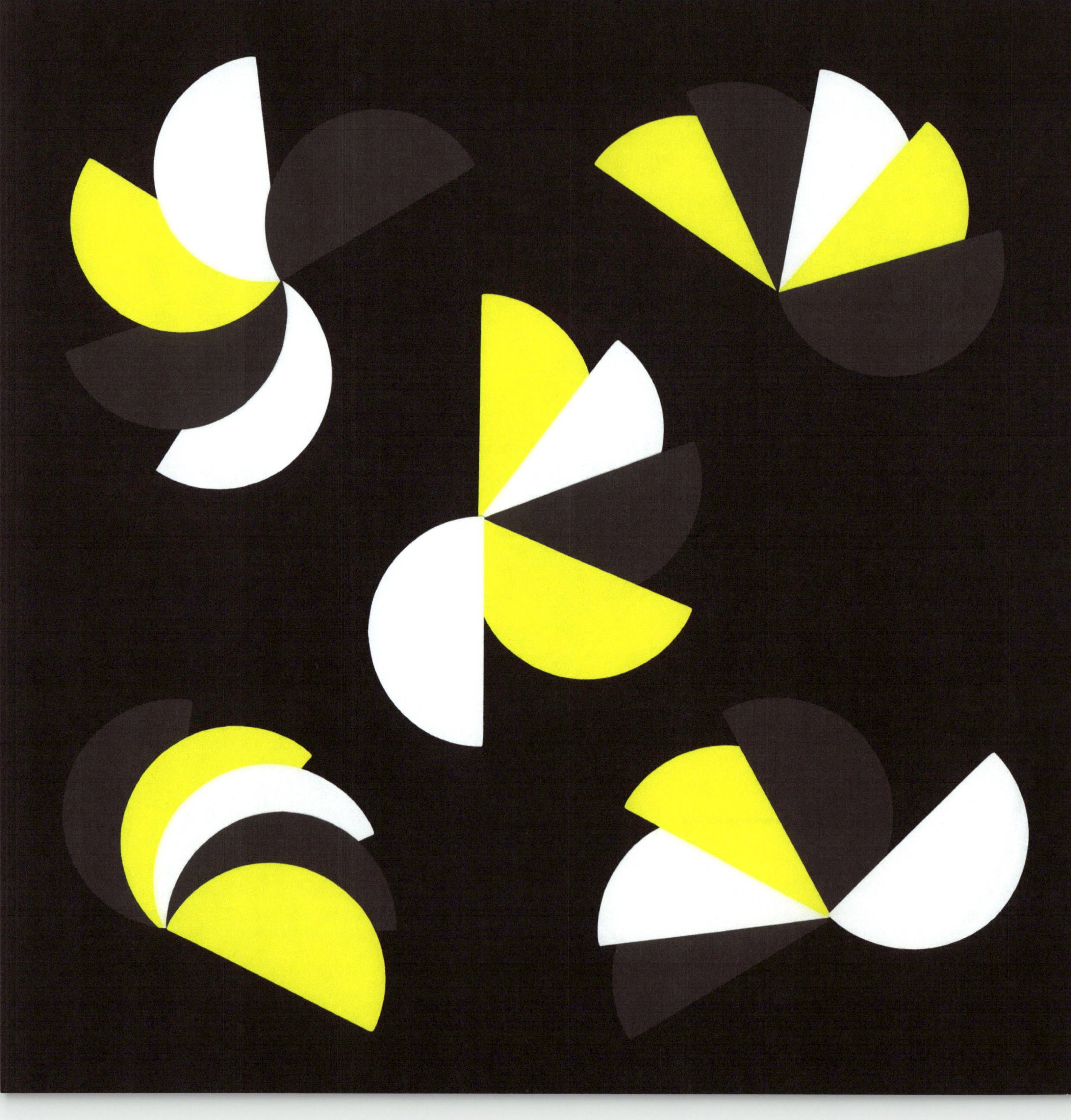

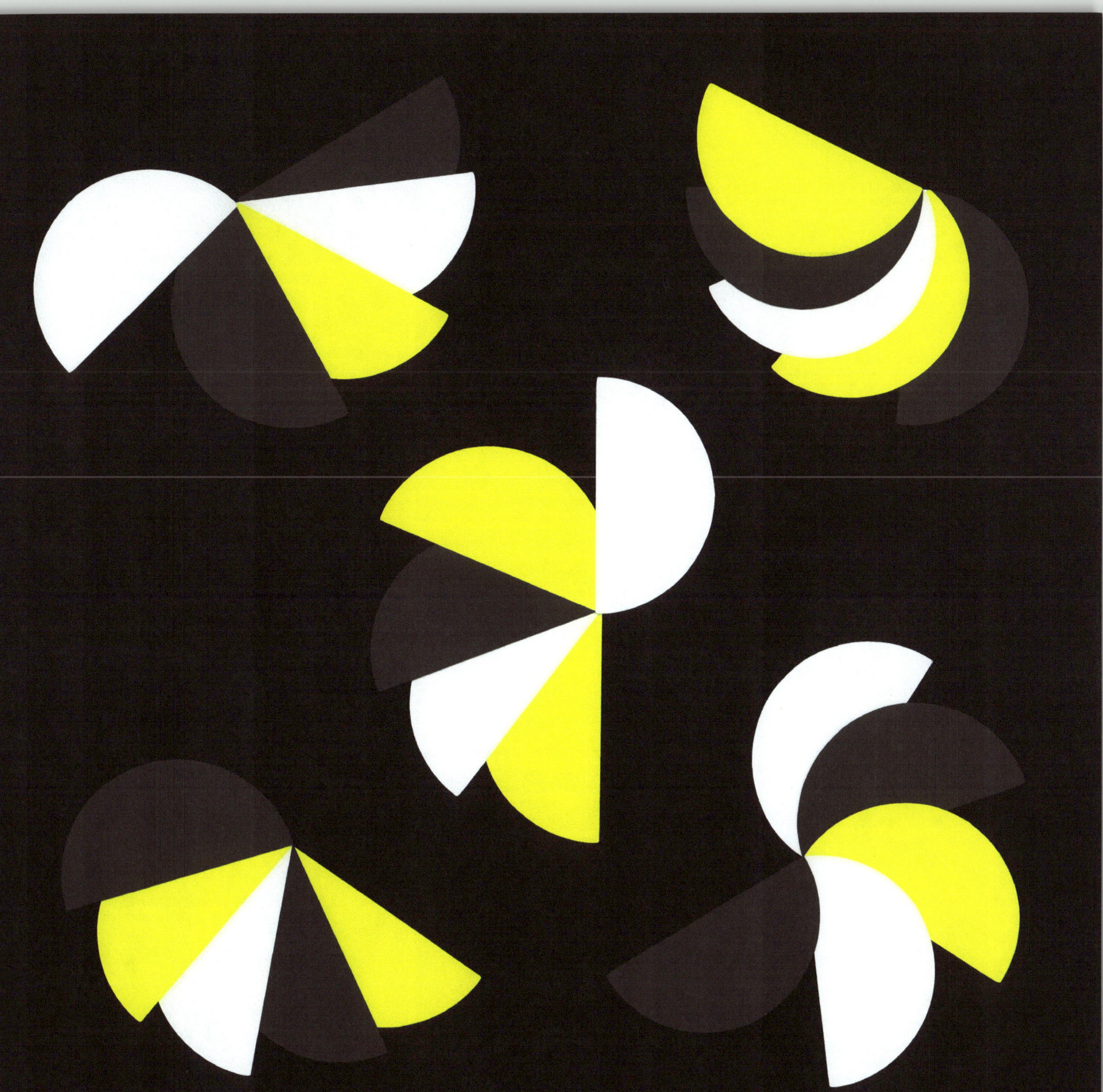

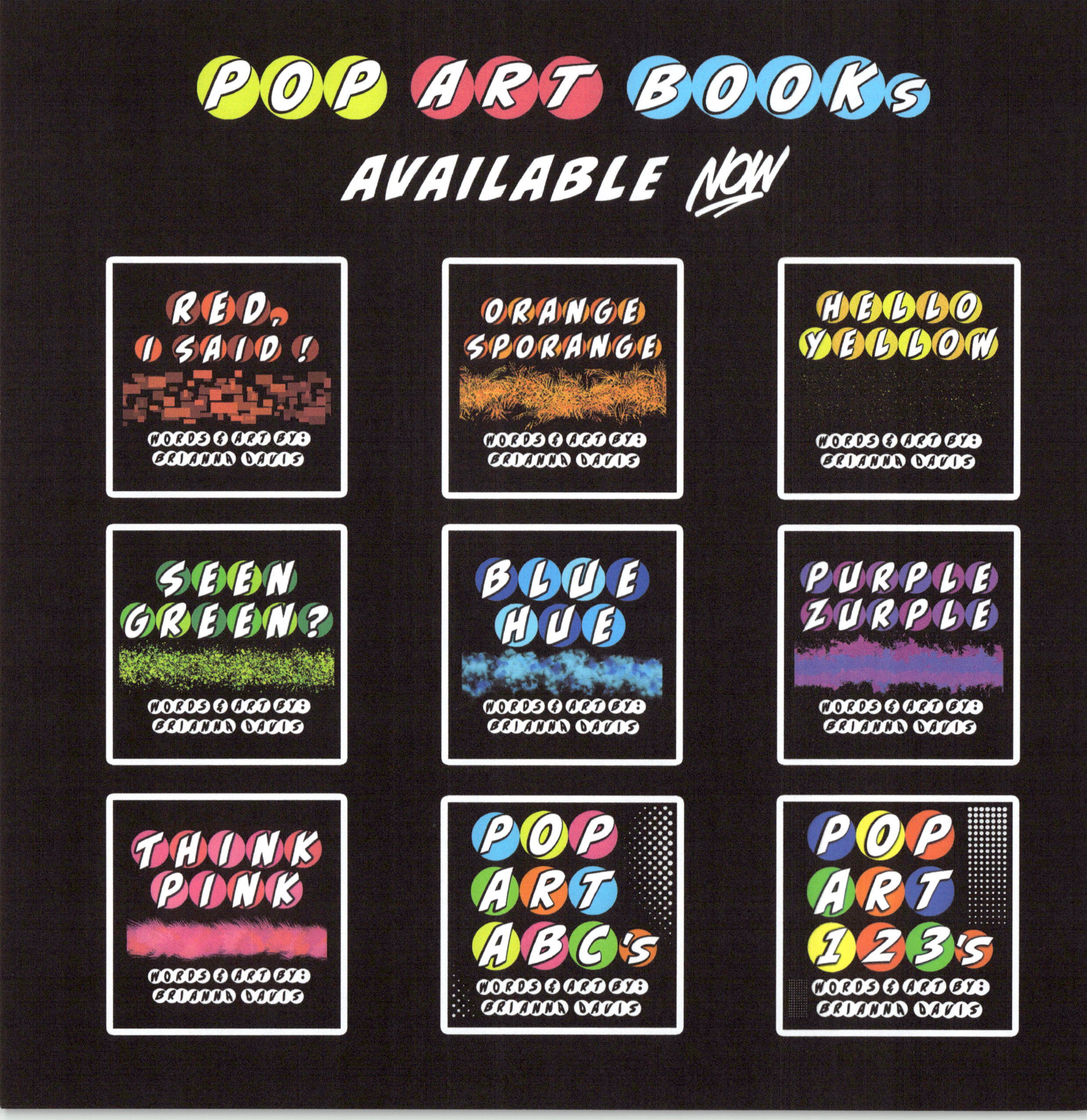
POP ART BOOKs
AVAILABLE NOW
RED, I SAID!
WORDS & ART BY: BRIANNA DAVIS
ORANGE SPORANGE
WORDS & ART BY: BRIANNA DAVIS
HELLO YELLOW
WORDS & ART BY: BRIANNA DAVIS
SEEN GREEN?
WORDS & ART BY: BRIANNA DAVIS
BLUE HUE
WORDS & ART BY: BRIANNA DAVIS
PURPLE ZURPLE
WORDS & ART BY: BRIANNA DAVIS
THINK PINK
WORDS & ART BY: BRIANNA DAVIS
POP ART ABC's
WORDS & ART BY: BRIANNA DAVIS
POP ART 123's
WORDS & ART BY: BRIANNA DAVIS

www.ingramcontent.com/pod-product-compliance
Lightning Source LLC
Chambersburg PA
CBHW051824210526
45473CB00005B/1732
9781954475304